I0099219

Activating the L.E.A.D. in Leadership

Lisa Nanches Jackson

Elshamar Desktop Publishing

Copyright © 2017 Lisa Nanches Jackson

All Rights Reserved. No part of this book may be reproduced or utilized in any form or by any means, electronic or mechanical, including photocopying, recording, or by any information storage and retrieval system, without permission in writing from the publisher.

ISBN 13: 978-0-9748006-3-9

FOREWARD

Countless books, publications, and periodicals address the ongoing mission to become better leaders, thereby continuing the rhythm of successful leadership. Great leaders are open to continued learning and encourage others to become their best in more than one sphere of influence through study, research, and rehearsing what other great leaders have done. With relentless conviction from personal, governmental, and Christian leadership experience, Lisa R. N. Jackson heralds that all leaders must maintain integrity and character as we lead others. Her approach to leadership is that we bring our authentic self to the table and establish trust with those we are leading. **Activating the L.E.A.D. in Leadership's** 3-part series admonishes leaders to acknowledge blind spots, weaknesses, and challenges that impede effective leadership in contemporary times.

Secure leaders are passionate in developing leaders around them for the success and continued growth in the organization. The practical applications at the end of each segment allow the "learning-leader" to be accountable. Accountability is as much practical as it is marketable in the 21st century. Leaders who make the commitment to lead by example and not through the positional power are in high demand, especially among millennials. Consequently, rethinking how we lead in the 21st century can be challenging but is necessary when addressing the needs of ever-changing demographic. **Activating the L.E.A.D. in Leadership** will motivate leaders to recalibrate and rebrand your leadership approach and style.

I sincerely recommend **Activating the L.E.A.D. in Leadership.** It will prove to be a how-to tool. It's creative, loaded with leadership applications yet profound in clarity and upward movement. If you are new in your leadership career, this is an excellent model to jump-start your journey. If you are an experienced leader, this tool will galvanize your authentic leadership style and approach.

Let's push the restart button on leadership to influence, impact, and add value to those who follow us! Continue as a learning leader, encourage others to be better than yourself (which is authentic leadership), and remain committed to the cause for which you are most passionate.

Leading on Purpose,

Dr. Wanda Frazier-Parker
Certified Coach, Speaker, Teacher & Trainer
Empowered For Living

This book is dedicated to my family (husband Carl, daughter Tierra, and mother Golethia. The tremendous love, support, and the confidence that you have shown me have been the wind beneath my wings. You consistently believe that I can do anything and now I do too! I would also like to thank my spiritual parents/pastors Bishop Alfred A. Owens, Jr. and Co-Pastor Susie C. Owens they have been tremendous role models and mentors. Special thank you to my contributors, Dr. T. Cedric and Coach Bobette Brown, whose support made this book possible.

This is the first of a three-part series. This series will be a necessary resource to add to every great leader's library.

1. **Activating** the L. E. A. D. in Leadership

2. **Igniting** the L. E. A. D. in Leadership

3. **Unleashing** the L. E. A. D. in Leadership

Preface

According to the Harvard Business social animals known for using their howl like a sophisticated instrument to keep their pack synced. But don't start barking orders at your team. Instead, as an alpha leader, keep your pack aligned with focused, emotionally-charged communication."

In some ways, GREAT leaders are like the Alpha wolf. They lead with their presence and their followers fall in line by choice.

Activating the **L. E. A. D.** in Leadership

Learner
Encourager
Authentic
Determined

There is a great debate about whether leaders are born or made, but I submit to you that there is no debate that if we are going to be effective we have to be intentional about leading. The author shares what she has gleaned, discovered and imparted through nearly 26 years of leadership.

> Are leaders born or made? This is a false dichotomy – leaders are neither born nor made. Leaders choose to be leaders.
> – Steven R. Covey

This book is meant to challenge the reader not to settle for being a good leader, but to continue to aspire to be great.

> Good is the enemy of great. And that is one of the key reasons why we have so little that becomes great." – Jim Collins

Great leaders are life-long **learners**. They are wise enough to know that relevant, impactful leadership is a journey and not a destination.

Great leaders are **encouragers**. They inspire with courage and confidence. They are purposeful in identifying and developing the seed of greatness that lies in those they lead.

Great leaders are **authentic**. They are sincere and serious about developing others. They treat people the way they want to be treated. They aren't wrapped up in their leadership positional power, they don't look down on others or pretend to be interested in their followers, and they are genuine.

> Leaders and followers create the power of leadership. Leaders offer direction and followers commit to it." – Warren Blank

Great leaders are **determined**. They are purposeful and unwavering in their commitment to their cause to influence, direct and guide others.

Author, Dr. T. Cedric Brown writes, **great leaders are life-long Learners.** They are wise enough to know relevant, impactful leadership is a journey and not a destination. They also know in order to increase their capacity to lead there are a few questions they must ask themselves.

1. Are you pushing yourself to learn something new when it comes to leadership every day? Or, are you just doing what you already know to do?

2. Are you stretching yourself to go beyond your comfort zone—beyond what you do well enough—and engaging in activities that test you and build new skills? Are you learning?

Remember, leaders who do what they already know to do, do not get better at what they do. They are not learning anything new.

Listed below are some helpful approaches to learning.

Self-assessment or Value Audit
Take an inventory of your unique talents and strengths. Also know your weaknesses, hopes, worries/fears, and goals. Becoming familiar

with these areas will give guidance to the direction you should take when considering growth strategies.

Others-assessment

Ask someone you trust (i.e. coach, pastor, mentor, etc.) what do they see as your unique abilities/talents, strengths, and weaknesses. One question to ask is, "If you invited me to teach a workshop/seminar what would be the subject/topic?"

Taking action

Great leaders are not afraid to learn by trial and error. Try something new. For example, implement a new speaking or teaching technique, learn a new skill, eat at a different restaurant, try new foods, take a class. Exposure is critical to leading effectively. Remember, you cannot lead beyond your level of skill, knowledge, pain, or experiences.

In conclusion, it does not matter your style of learning. What matters is doing more of whatever learning style that works best for you? "The Best Leaders are the Best Learners." -- Dr. T. Cedric Brown

> Leadership is developed daily, not in a day -- that is reality. John C. Maxwell

Five Things I Plan to do
implement on my
commitment to learning . . .

_____

_____

_____

_____

_____

_____

_____

_____

_____

_____

_____

_____

> "When the leader lacks confidence, the followers lack commitment."
>
> John C. Maxwell

Great leaders are Encouragers. There is something to be said about being an encourager that has a lasting effect on the recipient. I remember running cross-country in high school. I was preparing for the 4 x 4 relay race spring semester. I was not really a distance runner, but my coach told me that it would be beneficial to run year round. I can recall my first cross-country race at Cosca Park in Clinton, Maryland. As I recall, the course was quite challenging and all of the runners, so I thought, had left me behind. As I was nearing the last ¼ mile of the race, I was exhausted. However, I could hear my coach encouraging me to finish the race. I determined in my mind that I would not give up, but I would finish the race. As I was coming around the final bend mimicking a jogger/walker, I heard some rustling behind me. It was another runner coming up from the rear. I realized that I had the opportunity not to finish last. I could see my coach at the finish line waving his arms and yelling encouragement. He yelled, "dig deep and kick it out! You can do it!" The encouragement from my coach was like a boost of fuel. I do not know how I did it, because I was extremely tired. My slow trot became a sprint. I finished the race and I was not last!! The encouragement from my coach helped me pull something out that I did not realize I had in me. His encouragement gave me the confidence to defy the odds… a short distance runner, running a cross-country race and not coming in last place!

How often as leaders do we take the time to encourage those that we lead to push pass his/her identified limitations and to defy the odds? Encouragement can be like fuel to a person that is running on empty. When we look at the word encouragement, we see in the midst of the word another word, courage. Great leaders impart courage to those they lead. They do so by taking the time to look beyond the surface of those they lead, to the possibilities of what those that they lead can achieve. I challenge you to be the coach at the finish line encouraging those that you lead to "kick it out." Be that person that refuses to allow those you lead to be content with the status quo. Be that coach that precisely those you lead to be the best that they can be and beyond what they can see. – Lisa Nanches Jackson, MA/ MPT

Five Things I Plan to do to enhance my commitment to encourage those I lead . . .

_____

_____

_____

_____

_____

_____

_____

_____

_____

_____

Great leaders are Authentic. We are living in a generation where it is crucial to be genuine. If we are going to be effective leading cross the generations and gain the buy-in of the millennials we must be genuine.

Here is a story from a millennial that learned the importance of being an authentic leader. She writes, in 2002, I graduated from high school and in August of that year, I enrolled in college. I remember being so excited because it was my first time living away from home. I must admit that hitting the books was one of the furthest things from my mind and it showed. I went to school for an entire semester, my parents spent nearly $10,000 and I only earned one passing grade. My lack of focus turned what was traditionally a four-year trip into an eleven-year journey.

I eventually received a bachelor's degree and the determination to continue my educational pursuit to the doctoral degree level. Approximately two years ago, I had a conversation with a freshmen college student, who was a part of a youth group that I assist as one of its leaders. The student was at the end of her rope and had essentially decided that completing college was virtually impossible. As I sat and listened to the young lady, memories of my own experience began to flood my mind. I found myself at a crossroad. Do I listen with a sympathetic ear and just nod my head, or do I risk being transparent and share my story? Well I took the risk and decided to share my journey with the young lady. We talked for hours as she looked at me first in total amazement and then through the eyes of tears.

At the conclusion of our conversation, she decided to give college another try. Today, she is a rising junior at Shaw University who is determined now more than ever to finish what she started. It was then that I realized the true value of authenticity. My willingness to be authentic and share my experience toward this young lady's academic pursuit put her on a trajectory that would lead to graduation! – Tierra L. Nanches

We learn from the above-mentioned story that being an authentic leader will require us to be transparent and to be willing to take risks. The reality of leadership is there will be those that we lead who will be at the end of their rope, which will be on the verge of throwing in the towel and flooded with thoughts of defeat. An authentic leader can be that lifeline. Now do not get me wrong, we cannot save or enable people. However, there are times those we lead need a ray of hope. They need someone who is genuinely interested in guiding them and willing to be an example they can follow.

When leaders are authentic, it lets those we lead know that we are not perfect, although we should continue to strive for perfection. Authentic leaders let those they lead know that it is okay to ask for help and not only ask, but receive help. Donnie McClurkin, Jr., a pastor and gospel singer expressed authenticity clearly through two of his songs, "We fall down but we get up" and "I need you." The lyrics of both these songs reveal a genuine reality.

Five things I plan to change to be authentic in my leadership . . .

_____

_____

_____

_____

_____

_____

_____

_____

_____

_____

_____

_____

Great leaders are Determined. They are purposeful and unwavering in their commitment to influence, direct and guide others.

Coach Bobette Brown writes, what makes true leaders so strong-willed, resolute, and unrelenting? They understand the decisions they make today will impact generations to come. So, dispelling the thoughts of inadequacy is imperative in the character of a leader. Despite seemingly insurmountable tasks, leaders embrace a can-do attitude. They refuse to quit.

During a recent coaching session, I shared the power of determination by referencing the popular children's book, "The Little Engine that Could" by Watty Piper. The small train demonstrates the importance of determination, especially when it involves adding value to the lives of others. The small engine took on the responsibility of pulling a long train, which normally required the strength of a Freightliner, over a high mountain by indefatigable repeating its motto "I-think-I-can." This level of determination is analogous with the character of great leaders. They are indomitable to defy the odds against them. Their pledge to positively impact others will always drive them to confront impossibilities. – Author, Bobette G. Brown, MA

Five things I plan to do to switch my commitment to be determined in my leadership . . .

_____

_____

_____

_____

_____

_____

_____

_____

_____

_____

As a leader, you must realize that you teach what you know. Therefore, you must invest in yourself with studying and resources more than those you are assigned to develop.

You activate the lead in the leadership when you begin to invest in those you lead. When you invest you build morale, when you invest you will eventually receive a return on your investment. The return that you receive on your investment will be greater than your investment. Sometimes it is not about the monetary rewards, but rather an appreciation, accolades, words of affirmation. Sometimes, the intangible sincerity and authenticity of genuine appreciation can be a motivating factor for increased performance.

You activate the lead in leadership when you realize the power of influence. There is an old adage that says, "you attract more bees with honey than you do with vinegar". In short there is nothing wrong with the leader being nice. When a leader is confident in his or her ability to lead, they are not rude and insensitive. They do not have to lead from their personal title or position. Their ability will affect the character developed by the skills in those that he/she leads ultimately affecting his/her behavior. The do it because "I said so mentality" will not be effective.

Integrity is another essential characteristic of effective leaders. People will not willingly follow a person they do not trust. They may follow when they are being watched but they will not wholeheartedly follow.

We activate the lead in great leadership when **skill** is combined with **ability**.

I firmly believe that the foundation of great leadership begins with the leader knowing his/herself. The more you know about yourself and your abilities, the more equipped you will be to lead. It is important to know your strengths and your weakness. Knowing this information will allow the leader to make appropriate decisions and to lead with intentionality. The area that this author has found essential is **self-awareness.**

> John C. Maxwell said, in his book, The 360 Degree Leader, "to know how to get where you want to go, you need to know where you are. To get where you want to go, you need to focus on what you're doing now.

The journey of a great leader begins with self-awareness. The Oxford British & English

World Dictionary defines self-awareness as a conscious knowledge of one's own character and feelings. The more you know about yourself the more equipped you will become to lead others. Oftentimes people attempt to lead because they have been given the position, but being given a position of leadership doesn't automatically make you a leader. When people seek to lead from what I like to call positional power they are not effective. Have you become susceptible to leading solely from positional power? Do you find yourself pointing people to your position in order to get them to follow your direction? Leading from positional power is sort of like bad parenting. When the parent does not model effective living for his/her child but tries to parent by saying "do as I say and not as I do," It does not work well. When a person leads solely from positional power, they are essentially saying "do this because I'm the boss or do this because I'm the president." Therefore, it's not the person leading, it's the position directing. Conversely, when a person invests in his/herself to identify their strengths, their weaknesses and then to commit to doing what it takes to be competent, that person will lead from personal power. If this is you and you desire to be a great leader, you cannot be content with positional power.

> Steven Covey in his book Principle-Centered Leadership says "leaders with legitimate power are trusted, respected and honored. And they are followed because others want to follow them, want to believe in them and their cause, and want to do what the leader wants.

Self-Awareness

1. It refers to assessing your leadership style/temperament

   - Where you are now?

   - Where would you like to be in five years?

2. It requires exploring essential qualities of Great Leaders;

3. EQ – Emotional Quotient. According to the Cambridge Dictionary, the EQ is defined as a measurement of a person's emotional intelligence (their ability to understand their own feelings and the feelings of others).

4. LQ – Leadership Quotient. According to Dr. Keith Johnson, the leadership quotient is defined as a composite

measure of a person's leadership skills that positively influence people to join that person in achieving desired outcomes that benefit others.

5. Knowing whether you are a born leader.

Once we have embarked upon the journey of self-awareness, we then have to expand our focus to **developing others**.

> "A leader who produces other leaders multiplies their influences."
> John C. Maxwell

Developing Others

1. Requires that leaders articulate their expectations

2. Build authentic relationships that develop people

3. Allow people to work on upward mobility tasks, even when you are present

4. Challenge People – When we challenge people, we create capacity in the person that is being challenged.

5. Confront those that we lead in Love

6. Be willing to have Courageous Conversations

7. Adjusting to fit the developmental follower's style [Situational Leadership]

8. As John Collins says, it requires making sure that everyone is on the right seat of the bus. In other words ensuring that each person has the right position or role.

9. Being willing to explore John Maxwell's concept of Leading (360-degree Leadership by John Maxwell) - Think 360 – realize the value of followers

10. Realize when we develop the employee we develop our organization

11. Facilitate filling in the GAP – The GAP is the difference between where they are and where they need to go (assessing when it's appropriate to train and when it's more appropriate to educate)

The leaders of tomorrow will be identified and cultivated by the GREAT leaders of today. This can be achieved with intentional **succession planning**.

Essentially, when we talk about succession planning, we need to answer three questions. First, what is succession planning? According to the Business Dictionary, succession planning is identification and development of potential successors for key positions in an organization, through a systematic evaluation process and training.

In other words, succession planning is a process for identifying and developing internal people with the potential to fill key leadership positions in the organization.

Second, why do we need to plan for successors? Succession planning increases the availability of experienced and capable employees that are prepared to assume leadership roles as they become available.

Third, how do we begin the planning of a successor? We need to review the long-term vision and direction of the organization and develop a written policy that establishes principles, clarifies roles, and implements procedures in the event of a key role vacancy.

I have learned throughout my leadership journey the importance of developing principles. The principles that I have developed have been helpful to me and I hope that they are helpful to you too. The Oxford British & English World Dictionary defines a principle as a fundamental truth or proposition that serves as the foundation for a system of belief or behavior or for a chain of reasoning. It is important to realize that our methods of leading may change based upon those that we are leading.

However, there are some fundamental things that will prove effective no matter the follower.

Leadership Principles

★★★★★★

Practical Principle One

➢ When we cease to learn, we cease to be
relevant.

The reader's thoughts for putting this
Principle into practice . . .

Practical Principle Two

➢ Neither success, nor succession happens by accident, you must be intentional.

The reader's thoughts for putting this Principle into practice . . .

Practical Principle Three

➤ When leading, competence breeds confidence.

The reader's thoughts for putting this Principle into practice . . .

Practical Principle Four

- ➢ As leaders, we must model the behavior that we want to see.

The reader's thoughts for putting this Principle into practice . . .

Practical Principle Five

➤ Seek to lead from your personal and not positional power.

The reader's thoughts for putting this Principle into practice . . .

During my tenure as a leader, I have found that there are fundamentally three **Essential C's of Leadership.**

1. **C**ompetence – A Great leader must be competent. The Oxford British & English World Dictionary defines competent as having the necessary ability, knowledge, or skill to do something successfully. In other words, a great leader knows what to do to get the job done and if he/she does not know, they will find out.

> Positive personality traits, while often essential for success, constitute secondary greatness. To focus on personality before character is to try to grow the leaves without the roots." -- Steven Covey

2. Good Character – A Great leader must possess good character. According to Jill Schoenberg, a person that is considered to have good character exhibits attributes such as integrity, honesty, courage, loyalty, fortitude, and other important virtues that promote good behavior and habits. It has been said that character is how we act when no one is looking. A great leader has strong moral principles and can be trusted to be fair.

3. **C**ourage – A Great leader must have courage. The Oxford British & English World Dictionary defines courage as the ability to do something that frightens one; bravery. There are circumstances and situations that leader's face that require them to take risks. It takes courage to take risks. A Great leader does not allow fear to paralyze him/her; they turn their fear into fuel and forge forth.

I challenge you to activate the L.E.A.D. in your leadership and refuse to be comfortable with the status quo. Commit to learning all that you can and share all you learn with those you lead.

Give support, confidence, and hope to the followers of today and the leaders of tomorrow. Be willing to step outside of your comfort zone and be transparent, your authenticity will set you up for even greater success. The solution that will bring current leadership to a greater level is to seal your ability and skill with the determination to get better each day and to leave your followers better off than before they experienced your leadership. You are now ready to ignite the L.E.A.D. in your leadership. Learn the how in Volume 2 of this series.

www.ingramcontent.com/pod-product-compliance
Lightning Source LLC
Chambersburg PA
CBHW061757040426
42447CB00011B/2338

* 9 7 8 0 9 7 4 8 0 0 6 3 9 *